CW01066969

Spotlight Poets

A New Beginning

Edited by Sarah Marshall

Spotlight *Poets*

First published in Great Britain in 2004 by
SPOTLIGHT POETS
Remus House
Coltsfoot Drive
Peterborough
PE2 9JX
Telephone: 01733 898102
Fax: 01733 313524
Website: www.forwardpress.co.uk

SB ISBN 1 84077 115 1

Foreword

As a nation of poetry writers and lovers, many of us are still surprisingly reluctant to go out and actually buy the books we cherish so much. Often when searching out the work of newer and less known authors it becomes a near impossible mission to track down the sort of books you require. In an effort to break away from the endless clutter of seemingly unrelated poems from authors we know nothing or little about; Spotlight Poets has opened up a doorway to something quite special.

A New Beginning is a collection of poems to be cherished forever; featuring the work of twelve captivating poets each with a selection of their very best work. Placing that alongside their own personal profile gives a complete feel for the way each author works, allowing for a clearer idea of the true feelings and reasoning behind the poems.

The poems and poets have been chosen and presented in a complementary anthology that offers a variety of ideals and ideas, capable of moving the heart, mind and soul of the reader.

Sarah Marshall

Contents

The Authors
& Poems

June Waine

I was born in St Helens, Merseyside, but have lived in the small market town of Prescot in Merseyside since I got married in 1963. I have two grown up children, Neil and Carole. Unfortunately, my husband died after only four years and I never remarried.

Prescot is a very old town once well known for its watch and clock making and has a beautiful old church dating from before the 15th century.

I trained as a State Enrolled Nurse at Billinge Hospital near Wigan from 1960 to 1962 and then worked at Whiston Hospital near Prescot until 1964 when my son was born.

A year after my husband's death, I resumed my nursing career, working on medical and surgical wards, but I was happiest on the paediatric unit and retired from there in 1997 after 37 years.

Since my retirement I have kept busy and completed many courses, including computer skills, art and craftwork. I really enjoy painting in watercolours especially landscapes and still life, I also love to make my own greetings cards for family and friends.

I have been writing poetry for many years but have never belonged to any writers' group or had anything published. My favourite theme is memories and I have written several in a series called 'I Remember'. I have also done a few funny poems and quite a lot of a romantic nature.

There have been lots of people and events that have influenced the way I write. My mother was the biggest influence in my life with her love and understanding of everyone and everything around her. She had very humble beginnings but was a true lady.

Love Denied

It's 2am
She sits alone
Beside her silent
Telephone
Reluctantly now
She climbs the stairs
Wondering if
He thinks of her
Sadly she shakes
Her weary head
Longing for him
In her lonely bed
And in the darkness
Admitting her fears
She soaks her pillow
With bitter tears

It's 2am
He lies awake
Knowing his world
Is all a fake
Beside him the one
He took as a wife
Longing for she
Who changed his life
The woman moves
He's unaware
His heart aching
Yearning for her
But . . . he knows
He'll never be free
And lose this love
He needs desperately.

Moving Day

It seemed like a good idea at the time
Mulling it over
With a glass or three of wine
Pack up all my worldly goods
And move to pastures new
Try new start . . .
Yes, that's what I'll do

It seemed like a good idea at the time
Now I've lost all sense
Of reason and rhyme
It's all hustle and bustle
With boxes in piles
And the black plastic bags
Seem to go on for miles

It seemed like a good idea at the time
Now surrounded by chaos
I've lost track of time
I can't find the teapot
And I'm dying of thirst
Now it's started to tipple
Can it get any worse?

It seemed like a good idea at the time
What was I thinking . . . ?
Am I losing my mind?
Send the van away please
I've just had enough
Call the agent and buyers
And say it's all off
But wait . . .

Now that I'm here
In my brand new abode
And the moving van's gone
In a cloud up the road
The teapot is found
And it made a fine brew
I'm beginning to chill
I'm thinking it through

It seemed like a good idea at the time
It was . . . and I'm fine!

You

I want to know the whole of you
Where you go
What you do
Every minute of every day
What you're thinking
And what you say
When you sleep
And when you laugh
Or cry

To be a part of everything
Share with you
What life may bring
Whether times are good or bad
When you're happy
When you're sad
Ending your loneliness
Bringing you happiness
And love

I want to feel that I belong
To comfort you
When things go wrong
Sharing all your hopes and dreams
Be part of all your
Plans and schemes
Whether the path
Is narrow or wide
I'll walk it by your side
Forever

Her Hero

The child . . .
Remembers a youthful lad
Chasing her to the gate
Lifting her high
She'd almost fly
Squealing with delight

The girl . . .
Remembers a soldier boy
Going off to war
His letters said
Uncle 'torment' Fred
Would soon be home once more

The teenager . . .
Remembers a nervous groom
On his wedding day
Standing beside
His beautiful bride
Wow! It nearly blew her away

The woman . . .
Remembers a family man
Sailing to a new life
He said his goodbyes
With a tear in his eye
She'll never forget that day

The niece . . .
Remembers this gentleman
On whom she could depend
More like a brother
There'll not be another
Her pal, soulmate, and friend

Starting Out

I like you
And you like me
We've found each other
And we're fancy-free
I feel unhappy
When we are apart
For, how can this 'love-in'
Ever start?

I want you
And you want me
We like each other
It's very plain to see
Are we 'in love'?
We may have some doubt
But, won't it be fun
Finding out?

I am you
And you are me
We are each other's
Sanity
You share my joys
I feel your pain
Sharing, caring
We can only gain

So, if we start as friends
You never know
Love may blossom
From the seeds we sow.

The Bridesmaid

I remember . . .
Forty years today
A misty morn
A wedding day
A little girl
Dressed in blue
Bedecked in flowers
Of every hue
Posy held tight
In trembling hands
The happiest bridesmaid
In the land

I remember . . .
How her heart bound
When 'she' arrived
In that wedding gown
A vision in white
With radiant face
Passed on by
With a rustle of lace
Heart a'fluttering
The bridesmaid in blue
Escorted the bride
To her groom

I remember . . .
That little girl
How she felt
The wonder of it all
No picture dulled
No memory fade
But a lasting impression
On me . . . the bridesmaid
But most I remember
Though years pass away
The love I saw blossom
Forty years ago today

Do Not Weep

Do not weep
I am not gone
I am just a breath away
Waiting . . .
Till we are together again

Feel me in the sunshine
Warming your aching heart
Or, in the whispering breeze
Brushing away your tears
See me in every bloom
Smiling back at you
Hear me in a melody
Or in a child's laughter
Soothing your troubled mind

I am all around you
Falling in the gentle rain, or
In a snowflake
Washing away all your sadness
Speak of me
Not with weeping words
But in joy and happiness
For I am not gone
I live in your heart

My Thanks

Thank you . . .
For making her smile
And for the glow
On her face
If only for a little while

Thank you . . .
For easing her pain
And putting
A purpose
Back into her life again

Thank you . . .
For helping her cope
For boosting her
Confidence
And giving her hope

Thank you . . .
For showing you care
For lifting
Her spirit again
And for loving her

The Lady

She was a lady . . .
My mother
In all the world
There was no other
Who saw only good in everyone
Who never thought she'd done
Enough, or given her best
Never thinking herself
Any grander than all the rest

A real lady . . .
My mother
And knowing her
You'd soon discover
Her genteel soul and loving heart
Deep within, from a humble start
She had no aristocratic blood
No noble birthright
But a rich abundance of good

A special lady . . .
My mum
Sharing my dreams
And spurring me on
Always there when hope was spent
Building in me new confidence
And throughout life she strove
To leave my legacy
A wealth, a plethora of love

Jacqueline Selby Brooks

I have been interested in writing since childhood and while in senior school I wrote and illustrated a book about my cats. My English teacher, Mrs Smith, requested a copy, which she kept along with another little book I wrote, both of which are now lost to me.

Over the years I have written on and off but never did anything with my stories or poems. Then just under a year ago I started to write poetry fairly regularly and showed it to my husband Jim, he has been a great encouragement to me. I joined the Authorsden Website and the friends I have made there have also been encouraging with their reviews of my work. A number of my poems have also been published in our local newspaper and on their website.

I am retired, living in the beautiful North Yorkshire countryside with my husband and our four cats. Our respective children are scattered across the globe. Jim's two daughters, a grandson and granddaughter live on the beautiful island of Maui. My two daughters live in Hereford and Scotland with their families. I also have one son, four granddaughters and one great granddaughter, Sophie.

I do not stick to one particular theme in my poetry, some of it is inspired by childhood memories, some inspirational, reflecting my Christian beliefs. I also write about my cats and their antics. Nature and wildlife has very often been an inspiration to me. Sometimes I just have fun letting my imagination run riot! A few poems have had a romantic theme, or reflections of other emotions and events that have affected my life. One or two have been inspired by events in the news. One of my latest poems, 'Stroke' was born out of my work as a volunteer dysphasic speech therapist.

I Saw You Watching Me

I saw you
Watching me
Across that crowded room,
A stranger
That before I'd never seen,
My future bridegroom.

I looked at you
You spoke to me,
Chemistry sparked between,
We danced
And talked the night away,
Soulmates unforeseen.

Scandal
And jealousy,
From those who did not know
True love
Can happen at first sight
And continue to grow.

I know
Your thoughts,
You speak my mind,
So close
And inseparable,
Our hearts are entwined.

Your eyes
Probe my soul,
To you it lies bared,
Drawing out
All the secret longings
That no one else has shared.

I opened
My heart again,
A vulnerable mess,
You took it
And now it's overflowing
With your love and tenderness.

You renewed
My broken heart,
Restored my confidence,
Your love
Instilled new life within
My soul sings with eloquence.

As lovers
And best friends,
For two decades and more,
We'll remain
Forever sweethearts,
Whatever life may hold in store.

You Came Into My Life

You came into my life at a very bad time,
And took a chance,
On my fractured heart
That was beginning to harden
And where cynicism had set in;
My tears had dried up, I'd cried them all out,
My life was a desert
Where no roses could bloom,
But love is a healer,
And you gave me that,
You turned on a tap and my tears came back,
They flowed like a river,
And this time for joy,
Softening my heart
And washing right out
The clutter of bad memories, rejections hoard.
You gave me my life back
And helped me to move on,
To grow and to flourish
In this garden of love.
No bitterness or anger in my heart can live,
It's too full of love
For sorrow to stay,
You fill it right up
And all I can say,
I'll love you my darling forever and a day.

Rambling

Down narrow country lanes
Lined with overhanging trees;
Cool, shady leafy tunnels
That only dappled light fills.

Quiet woodland glades
A bluebell-filled heaven;
Fairy rings and butterflies
And pretty red squirrels.

Then out into the sunlight
Of the open patchwork fields;
The lushness of the meadows
Of the valleys and the hills.

Homes clustered in the valley
Built of mellowed sandstone;
Weather-worn and seasoned
Drystone walls built with skill.

Sweet-smelling meadowsweet
With creamy florets,
And honeysuckle hedgerows
Perfuming warm summer air.

The meadowlark up high
Sings a very sweet song;
And the yellowhammer flirts
To lead the walker on.

Gypsy ponies grazing
Tethered near the road;
Waiting for their owners
To bring their oats by.

A tan-coloured cow
Quietly chewing on her cud;
Rests her chin on the wall
And dolefully gazes on.

Trout leaping in the beck
To catch the mayfly;
Sparkling water droplets fall
From rainbow-hued sides.

Rambling through the countryside
A pleasant day is spent;
Observing nature's beauty
Till the evening sun is set.

Apple Pie

Up to my eyes in cooking apples.
A bountiful harvest from
a friend's orchard garden.
Coring and peeling,
(time stealing)
Cut into large chunks,
simmer gently, lightly sweetened.

Mmmm! What an odour
it makes the mouth water!

Up to my elbows in apple pie pastry,
careful to use a very light touch
must keep it nice and flaky.
How many will I make,
a couple of dozen?
Only one for Eric
cos he's diabetic,
two for Margaret and Reg,
(she gave me some veg.)
and maybe Heidi and Matt
they would like one or two.
A dozen for the coffee morning
to fund our local Air Ambulance.
Got to find room in the freezer too,
to keep Jim supplied, while I'm away!
Oh dear, have I kept one for me?
Roll out the pastry and fit to the dish,
fill with apple and top with a lid.
Crimp the edges, sugar the tops,
then bake in the oven until
a rich golden brown.

Mmmm! What an odour
it makes the mouth water!

Serve with Devonshire cream
or one scoop (or three!)
of real Cornish ice cream.
Mmmm! The odour has taste
and it's so very moreish.
So what - if it goes to my waist?
Forget about diets and pass me that dish!

Cats' Toys

C ats' toys are simple things
A paper ball or a piece of string,
T he draught excluders that look like snakes
S ome imagination is all it takes.

T hat cushion that moved
O h, it must be killed if not disproved,
Y arn that hangs from crochet hooks
S oap bubbles and pages turned in books.

A spider running across the floor
R eflections on the wall or door
E verything within reach of a paw.

S hoelaces that really should be untied
I maginary mice that are often spied
M aking puss cats really wide-eyed,
P aper bags and cardboard boxes
L et cats invent their own Fort Knoxs'
E ach safe to dream of chasing foxes.

T o pounce and chase is such great fun
H appiness is in a madcap run
I n climbing trees and snoozing in the sun,
N ecklaces dangled, their paws to tease
G iving chase to leaves blown in the breeze
S uch simple things a cat will please.

I Want!

(Sammy Jo's lament)

She's as mad as a hatter
Her eyes spittin' fire
As she stands here
Just screaming at me.

'I want to go *out!*
I want to go *play*
In the garden
Not tomorrow, *today!*

You just sit here all day
On that wretched machine
I'm neglected, forgotten
Do you *hear* what I say?

I want *you* to come too
Give me some of your *time!*
Pay attention to *me,*
Forget about rhyme.

I want to go play,
It's a nice sunny day
And if you don't come too
I *will* phone the RSPCA!

I'll tell them you neglect me
How you treat me so mean,
That you love your computer
Much more than you love *me!*

If you don't come out *now*
I might run *away,*
And you won't see me
Till the *end* of today!

Come play in the grass,
I'll roly-poly for *you!*
Just for *your* enjoyment
(And mine too!)

You can make me a necklace
Of a pretty daisy chain,
And I promise to wear it
Until I lose it *again!'*

House Martins

The house martins are gathering
for pre-flight instruction,
lining up and discussing
their youngsters' induction;
The last of the fledglings
are trained in flight patterns
and take-offs and landings
and practising tight turns!

They squabble and chatter
all night and day long,
'We've got to get fatter,
soon it will be time to be gone.'
They are planning their route
and departure morn,
all fledglings must be ready
to set off at dawn.

There is a long journey ahead
over sea and land,
with many a danger to dread
from gunfire, and netters who stand
waiting to trap the unwary bird,
attempting to rest their poor tired wings.
Over the Camargue, flying too low
down to Earth, the trapper will bring.

The end of our summertime
is their signal to leave,
for a warmer and much sunnier clime.
Abandoning their nests under our eaves,
off to the African continent they fly.
The strong and the fit
will make it, bye and bye.
They are not the kind to give up or quit.

Spotlight Poets

I will miss them while they are gone,
their constant chatter at night
and their aerial antics all day long,
they are always a wonderful sight.
Now I know winter is not far away
so I will look forward once more
to next year, and that lovely May day
when their return heralds, spring, as before.

Stroke

My mind is clear, just as sharp as a tack,
Though my words may come out front to back.

And I am not deaf, I still can hear
So please don't shout at me my dear.

I understand every word that you say,
Even though I may be having a bad day.

The stroke has affected my speech and my tongue,
And on certain words my tongue may get hung.

They may come out jumbled, to you make no sense
But that does not mean that I am daft or dense.

Though my communication skills are impaired,
Do not assume with them my faculties are compared.

Please don't talk down to me and my feelings ignore,
I am still the same person that I was before.

Please try to understand the frustrations I feel,
I need patience, encouragement and time to heal.

Stephen Leake

I currently live in East London where I work as a teacher having moved here in 1992 as a graduate of the Birmingham Conservatoire. I have always had an interest in poetry in its many forms and have written since childhood.

It is only recently since the end of 2003 that I have started to dedicate more time to my interest. I have already published a slim volume entitled 'Ten Minutes Only', and I am looking forward to seeing my poem 'Somewhere' published by Forward Press in May (to be included in 'Whispers On The Wind').

My earlier poems are autobiographical, dealing with scenes from childhood, adolescence and the north-west area I grew up in. I was fortunate enough to grow up in Blackpool and have drawn on the town itself and the Lake District - to which I was a regular visitor - as inspiration for my writing. The sea, water and natural images are key themes that weave their way in and out of my poems.

I am exploring new territories in my current work; my voice being more distinct as I explore simple observations of people, emotions and everyday events. I believe that I am identifying with the reader on a personal level and hope that everybody can gain something from my poems. I enjoy writing for a general audience; friends, family and, in some cases, for my students specifically. Communication is the key to all poetry, on whatever level.

I would like to thank Forward Press for giving me the confidence lift with my poem 'Somewhere' and also Andrew Ward and Andrew Martin who have and will continue to be invaluable as editors, critics and friends.

Five O'Clock Snowstorm

Self-perfected,
That sudden twisting riot
Of sentiment and
Semi-permanence. A swift ritual
Of cleansing; a doctor's smile.

It worked completely. The lightning
Thrown in for good measure,
The sudden gathering force
Of orchestral proportion
Resolving in the middle air.

Fox arrived, then left.
An afterthought flicked from the frame
An ellipsis . . . soon filled
By the faint hissing -
The cleansing again. Gone.

I felt complete in those six minutes
Amongst the exaggerated orange on white -
Behind the stippling, scattering frenzy.
We were all involved. Everyone.
Those minutes held us together -
Engraved our histories.

But now, the drowning rain
Disperses; jolts the purposeful shapes
And leaves passages -
Empty footprints for us to walk in -
And take the place

Of the snow.

Dora's Field

When did that field arrive?
Did he plant it for you?
Scraping. Stooping to embed each furtive bulb.
Perhaps it was always there;
The flowers diminutive. Unperverse.
Innocuous friends. Scrutinising.

March breath, sharp, as a photo's edge
Cuts the scene to a muddied stone
Where I posed. Strengthening the view
Of romantic rock, youth and wild
Daffodil, bending at each elbow.
An idyll - almost.
Was I in the field when the shutter closed?
Or beyond it; at the water's ledge?
Nevertheless we were dragged by the cold
To the ghosts of cows who stared
Right through us.

Did you too observe them?
Did they catch you in their maudlin gaze as you
Traversed the field. *Their* field

Lost in a cow's dream?

Being

The dead arm awakes.
Reaches for the clock,

Feels the forever world -
As sensitive as a new wing.

Irretrievable moments spiral.
Travelling, whirring

As gnats above familiar water.
Steam rises arrogantly

From concrete. Undead. Motions matter.
The twist of an unfed cat.

The moss expanding on the
Unglossed sill. All join in.

Sun rises. The thrush
Becomes a fan on a yellow lawn.

And behind a bamboo screen
A neighbour's tears flow

Like wine from a box.
Into this.

Not knowing
But being.

Awakening

What are these self-contained moments
Which hide, then appear and dash
Over the blue ridge?
Can they ever be slowed? - Held longer
Than an ice cube on winter's tongue?

To answer this, you must first
Breathe the fumes of the crushed basil,
Face the rain with a December hangover
Then listen. Listen to the scissored
Hands of a distant clock
Cutting the hours from our lives.

Shaping It

The road runs in the wrong direction.
The rain attempts to fill the lake.
Communication is silent, without language.
An agitated wind bowls over the surface,
The distracted light bounces off an awkward stump.
And the words? - They retain their white knots.

I seem to hide within them like
Gnats performing in familiar shades,
Sometimes formed. Sometimes not.

They are not here today. They're under the lid
Taut as piano strings waiting to be plucked
From air or simple melody.

I move the pen. But the words have gone away.

Drifting Off

Separated thoughts, fasten.
Central heating kicks itself. Finds its pitch.
Electricity treads water in a new womb.
Outside, the barbecue tolerates the rain.
We hear it. Obliging.

'Night,' I say. 'Night.' Again.
My words lean over a grey cliff.
Something explodes beneath.
Body stutters. You enter.
And leave.

You're already there. Submerged.
I wait for the door.
A face appears. Stone-blurred.

I don't know.
I don't know.
But follow

Like breath on morning's mirror.

Closing Time

There's no message here in the park's
Rented silence. Just a scene.
The ineffectual air toys with itself
Discreetly, in purple corners.

Land lies closed.
The shadows are giving up;
Grass becomes hard with frost,
And brittle adolescence.

Domestic complexities have
Worked overtime. Gone beyond the rails.
A grey child ambles with a sceptical dog.
The regular man with his night-bags
Steals a bench.

These allegiances will always continue.
But now, a dusky cough draws up beyond this place,
And the space where love and loyalties
Slide, makes way.

For tomorrow's key.

Mahalia's Sunflower

Yellow (loud with weeping), was
Your second choice.
You have it there. Beneath
Your flatly tuned smile
Which slides down your pencil.
You hear the voice somewhere behind
The aperture; guiding the light and your thoughts.

Your black eyes heed the pre-seeded spirals
Which carve their own, tight circumferences.
Drugged on a limb, you find a lost leaf,
You work to lift it to your own page.
Momentarily your ripening thoughts flutter to the window
And back to the lead. Settling.

You track and work the grain to life;
Strip the petals from your glass mind
And smudge each potent sepal into itself.
Then hand it in. A simple, searching stencil, on
Life.

You turn away,
Scrutinise the window and humourless January rain
And catch your flower.

Flapping on a print
Behind a closed door.
On the skyline.

Hermit-Hunt

The promenade has ceased arguing.
We are together. Mother and son.
Keen-faced against the cold.
Gripping our purpose.

Sandflies have retreated with
Summer's demeanour. Crouching, stilled
In some green-cream shelter.
(Last century's moulding).

The sea disappoints our tableau;
Foil band running against the skyline.
Worm-skinned, sand-turned silence
Crumples the moment.

The greyness persists. Even now.
The pool, looms; rancid-stained.
Pebbles sigh as they are shifted.
Lifted by mother and son.

A squeal. A tight-necked balloon-shriek
Pops the image.
The crab is taken. A sinister pleasure,
Weeping in a plastic bucket.

Signs

The end of the line, literally.
No gesture, no wave, no blunt admission
In that unanswerable afternoon.
Can't remember speaking; just a
Sepia-bruised moment on
The wrong side of a door.
The martins screamed submissions
Against the cool platform's draught.
It could have been Ilkley, though not too sure now.
(The sandstone walls, a board not giving detail,
A distant curlew unfolding the moor's air).

It remains as unclear as a scalded tongue.
I can see you slipping over the steel
Skyline.
Unzipping the landscape en-route
With the rain now bursting.
Or was it applauding?

Together, Sunday

The afternoon has shrunk.
The mind's tongue is tasting tomorrow.
It is exact as new breathing.

The books are prepared.
The texts have been read and stacked.
A handful of light composes with rain.

The freshly sliced moments are arranged.
The confused starlings are now in rows.
The mists of secrets have evaporated.

A formless man drifts by, unmarked.
The half-filled pen allows itself
To shape this page. This poem.

The Uninformed

Here we are,
Where hoods slide up silently -
Over shoulders narrowed
With scant concerns.
The night squats on a red bench
Surrounded by stars
With criminal smiles.
Their thoughts run like
Films not yet played;
Books not yet written
And old rooms with new doors.
We have prepared for them,
With their exaggerated gestures
(The hand-crossing, the thrusting
Veined necks), tense as the night.
They deny our existence;
Peering through leafless trees
Which shake the gloom with shame.
And empty air.

Risk-Take

Behind closed lids you'll see the route;
The pristine coastal road
No longer impassable.
Drive out from the cranium's snow and
Park by your motionless sea.
Let go. Breathe tenacity
Like the premature beech leaf (self-torn),
Tackling the white wind.

Raise a hand to the decaying, compacted
Streets, with their flashing murderous lights;
Steer swiftly through these perplexed routes of
(Seeming) normality, sheltered under one
Disgruntled roof.

Then discontinue. Reflect.
Observe your Sunday supplement home,
Your modest boat, moored in middle-England
And stare them both out, like a crumpled stray.

It's your 'now or never' moment.
The provincial sky is falling fast.
Take it now. Go. Or your today will remain today.

And your tomorrow also.

Losing Touch

Somewhere, we parted.
Left on that coarse sulphurous

Strand which knits the November
Twilight to the skyline.

The exact moment lost
In certain breaths of disregard -

As if the moon, nail-clipped
Had chosen its spot on the night's carpet.

Chosen its own distance, from
That too familiar star.

You're out there hanging;
A cloud over low water,

An embarrassed kettle waiting to whistle,
A letter, unfranked.

But for the moment,
The phone withholds its own numbers,

The computer restarts, again.
And the pen falters.

All points, withdrawn.

Patricia Adele Draper

I was born and raised in Melbourne, Australia, but now live in Kent. I wrote my first poem at the age of eleven and by twelve I was having it published. When I was young, I wrote about many things I did not really understand. Now I write about my own experiences and what I see around me. My belief is that poets are artists who paint pictures with words instead of paint. During my years as a young mother I didn't write but from the age of thirty-five or so, I have written constantly. It is wonderful to look back on the poems I wrote as a child and see how my life has changed with experience. The more complicated my life became the simpler my poetry became.

Religion was a very dominant part of my upbringing and it has left me with a deep-seated faith that comes out at times of stress or great need, such as when our son died at the age of fourteen years after being severely disabled from birth. Poetry with a religious leaning has always been part of my repertoire.

By profession I am a teacher who returned to study and gained three further degrees in history after turning fifty. This made me a qualified historian as well but I am once more working in education in Kent. Many fellow poets will recognise my need to carry a notebook and pen wherever I go because once a verse or rhyming couplet enters my head I must write it down or it will drive me crazy, even in the middle of the night.

My wish is that others get as much pleasure reading my poetry as I do composing it.

Strawberry Snow

Along Rochester's Northgate, up to the cathedral,
There stands a row of flowering cherry trees.
In spring they are attired in tutus of rosy pink
And they become a Mecca for the bees.
In summer they are green, giving shelter from the sun,
Shading the quaint teashop selling ice creams,
For panting dogs and owners, a respite from the heat,
And schoolboys, as they dream their summer dreams.
In autumn the leaves turn subtly, vivid gold and russet,
Before the wind brings them to the ground.
They pile in crunchy mounds along the cobbled path,
Children rustle through them, tossing them around.
Winter brings frost and snow, painting branches white
And in the gloom the trees stand stark and bare,
Underneath the surface changes are taking place,
Nature's cycle of life is working there.
Suddenly it's spring again, with sunny days so fair,
Those frothy blossoms once more deck the trees.
After reaching the pinnacle of their spectacular short stay
They become a strawberry snowdrift, on the balmy breeze.

Rochester's History

Its long, cobbled High Street
And meandering narrow lanes,
Bear silent witness to centuries long past.
Other towns have modernised
With skyscrapers reaching tall,
But Rochester Town's history will last.
Within the castle confines,
Behind the crumbling walls,
History is relived every night,
With ghostly spectres hovering
And dancing 'neath the moon,
Illuminated by silvery, lunar light.
As people tread the pathway
'Tween castle and cathedral,
Walking upon ancestors long past.
Contemplating those long gone,
Living on in them today,
Through whom Rochester's history will last.

Snowfall In High Street, Rochester

'There's snow on the bathroom window,'
Said he, as he stood on the stair.
I said, 'It wasn't there early in the day.'
I got up from my cosy chair.
Then I went to the lounge room window
And threw open the curtains wide.
I gasped with surprise and wonder at
What was happening down there, outside.
There were snowflakes coming down softly,
But what made us stop and stare,
They were not melting on contact,
But settling and gathering there.
Because the street is so narrow
And all the buildings so tall,
It's rare for snow to fall in High Street,
It doesn't happen often at all.
It all looked so pristine and lovely,
At least for a minute or two,
It was all marked with wheels and footprints
When the evening traffic rolled through.
It was still there early next morning,
So much of it had turned into slush.
We won't forget the incredible sight
Of snowfall in High Street, in a rush.

Heaven's Seed

The sky was leaden,
Grey and frustrated.
Then, in a coupling with Mother Earth
The tension grew to glorious orgasm
And Heaven spilled its precious seed,
To fall in frosted flakes.
It covered Mother Earth
And lay like fluffy marshmallow,
Blanketing the fertile soil.
Then, Heaven sent its sun
To warm the frosted blanket.
Out of the pristine coverlet grew
Two of Earth's premature daughters,
Both shy and green of eye,
Garbed in virginal white.
Mother Nature named them
Snowflake and Snowdrop,
Divine harbingers of spring.

Our Brave Soldier

You won't grow old like the rest of us,
No wrinkles will furrow your brow.
You'll stay forever young and strong,
Frozen in time somehow.
Not forgotten by those who loved you,
We will carry you in our hearts.
To be reunited in some future time
As each one of us departs.
Sleep in peace until then, our soldier.
Wrapped warm in God's good grace.
Until once more we embrace you
And look on your beloved face.

You are missing from family gatherings
But we speak often, as if you were here,
And we leave a place at the table,
Each Christmas, when we feel you near.
On each special Remembrance Day
We polish your medals with pride
And recall for young family members
The reasons our brave soldier died.
For now, we gaze at your image,
Standing tall and proud, off to war.
We join you in your sepia dreaming
'Til we can embrace you once more.

Owen's Song

When you see a dark-eyed daisy
First thing at the dawning,
With sparkling dew upon its face,
Blinking in the morning,
Think of me.

When you see a dainty butterfly,
With a life so fleet and fragile,
Remember how I used to be
And how I used to smile.
Think of me.

As all nature's finest treasures,
My life was a fleeting spark,
But with my love and patience,
I hope I left my mark.
Think of me.

I have gone before you,
But when you all come after,
I'll meet each one at Heaven's gate.
You'll hear my bubbling laughter.
Remember me.

The Pilgrim

A young man climbed the mountain
This morning, to Assisi town.
A bedroll and pack upon his back
And garbed in a habit of brown.
Not one word passed between us,
But I saw on his cherubic face,
The exhilaration he was feeling,
Arriving at this glorious place.
I know not from whence he came
And I know not where he will go,
But when he prays at the tomb of St Francis
His young face will be all aglow.
Perhaps he comes to beg shelter
From his brothers, the friars in brown.
They'll feed his body and nourish his soul
Within the walls of Assisi town.
He arrived as I was leaving,
So I have an inkling of what is in store,
But to the backpacking Franciscan friar,
I'm sure 'twill mean even more.

Dawn

Risen from the depths of darkness,
Like a jewel in the night.
Spreading crystal, prism fingers,
Changing darkness into light.

Like opening a box of magic,
Standing breathless, wait to see.
Sun peeps through its spreading fingers,
Awakening birds up in the tree.

Except the birds of night and gloom,
The sun is calling them to rest.
Wearily they fold their pinions
And settle down in cosy nest.

Reflections At Midnight

Over the crest of the hill at midnight,
On one of those crisp, clear winter's nights,
There in the middle of the ink-black sea,
Reflections of the highway lights.

Shimmering deep in the jet-black water,
Wide hazy pools of soft mellow light.
Gently ebbing to and fro with the tide,
On that crisp, clear winter's night.

My eyes moved out to the horizon,
Drawn to a gilded bird in flight.
A wingless bird, its jewelled reflection,
A golden orb of lunar light.

Grey Day

The sea looked like an elephant's back,
An expanse of wrinkled, moving grey.
Merging in with the sky above
And the road, as it snaked its way.
The day was hot, oppressive and dull.
Its mood was grey and so was mine,
As I watched from the window, dusty, grey,
Of the grey train crawling down a dull grey line.

Shanghai Cat

Thin and bony, very wary,
Seems to know the world is scary,
The Chinese cat perched on a Shanghai wall.
Treading slowly with great care,
He seemed to be quite aware
Of the danger, perchance that he might fall.

Not for him the silken cushion
Or the silver bowl with luncheon,
Just the fear of being eaten if he's caught.
So he steps lightly, with great care,
To venture low he would not dare.
To survive another day his only thought.

The Robin

I've been hearing your song
For ever so long,
From the other side of the wall.
But I saw you today
In your vivid array,
As you warbled your happy call.

Atop a leafless tree,
Looking down at me,
You trilled your message of spring.
Your red throat a'throbbin',
My small friend the robin,
Made me and the world want to sing.

The Heavens Wept

The heavens wept on Golgotha
The day Lord Jesus died,
And Peter heard again His words,
Three times He was denied.

The temple curtain rent in two
And the sky grew dark and black.
Thunder rolled around the Earth,
But He promised He'd be back.

In the Garden of Gethsemane
They placed Him in a tomb
But He rose on Easter morning,
Glorious fruit of Mary's womb.

And He shall live for evermore,
Through every coming age.
We can write our own small part
On Heaven's Holy page.

Help Me Lord

Help me Lord to do thy bidding,
Guide my feet through all my days.
Help me to follow your example,
As I raise my voice in praise.

Help me Lord to bear my burdens,
Quietly, without complaint.
Understanding others' troubles,
Giving myself without restraint.

Help me Lord to use my talents,
To make the world a better place.
Give me love and understanding,
For each creed and every race.

Help me Lord to listen always,
Keep a pure and open heart.
To receive your word Lord Jesus,
Always there to do my part.

Help me Lord to be the person
That I know you'd want me to.
Use my heart, my head, my hands,
To live and love and work for you.

Help me Lord to keep my footsteps
On the straight and narrow way,
And rejoicing, bring me home,
On that final Judgement Day.

Around And Deep In Me

In the crimson of a sunset,
In the pale grey of dawning,
In the sudden fall of raindrops
That comes without a warning.
In the colours of the rainbow,
In the sparkle of the sea,
I see the wonders of the Lord,
Around and deep in me.

In shimmering fields of golden wheat,
In the azure summer skies,
In the innocence and frankness
Of a new-born baby's eyes.
Everywhere I care to look,
I'm sure that I will see,
The bounties of my loving Lord,
Around and deep in me.

My Ancestor

You were shrouded in the mists of time,
A shadow of the days long past,
But slowly, and with loving care,
Your story was revealed at last.
Slowly I uncovered you
And bared your soul for all to see.
Despite misgivings deep inside,
I hope that you approved of me.
I pried into your private life,
Revealing secrets long forgot.
Unveiling things you tried to hide,
Telling a past you'd rather not.
Curiosity brought me first,
Soon replaced by a sense of pride.
I live now because you lived then
And you are forever by my side.

Jean Easson

My childhood was spent in Newbury, which at that time was quite a small market town. My interest in reading and writing stories and poetry started at quite a young age. After reading, 'Little Women', my dream was to be like Jo and write stories in an attic! However, the childish plan faded when I left home at sixteen years of age to start my nurse training. I am now nearing my fifty-second birthday and have been forced to give up my career within the caring professions due to osteoarthritis. Although this was rather a hard blow to accept, at least I have a little more time for writing.

It is said you should write about what you know and of course during a career spanning over thirty years, I have seen many changes. These changes are not only within health services but also in the lifestyle and social patterns of humanity. A great deal of my work reflects today's newsworthy events and hidden social issues, which many people prefer to forget about. Domestic violence, child abuse, mental health problems, are all on our doorstep and need to be discussed and understood. War may be closer than we think. We may learn about what others have suffered over our last fifty plus years of relative peace. So many avoidable, painful experiences suffered by so many.

There are times when I reflect on my childhood and family life with pleasure but, of course, some sadness. I am very lucky in that I have a wonderfully supportive husband and have a fantastic view of a very well-kept pretty garden that is maintained by the Essex Wynter Trust. This means even on painful days I am surrounded by beauty that can be most inspiring.

The Decision

I cannot cry, our child may hear,
what can I do? I love him dear.
He is always sorry, it's my fault
I cause him worry,
hence these assaults.
Tonight has been the worst so far,
can I escape, is the door ajar?
Is it my man or the ale talking?
Have I strength to start walking?
No screaming, it might wake our child,
she is busy dreaming,
and should not hear his bile.
The words full of hatred,
my mouth full of blood,
what happened to the man, I loved?

All quiet now, his anger spent,
tomorrow I must not relent.
No more, no more, I must be tough,
protect our daughter with my love.
She must not know the fear that I do,
I must find a hiding place from you.
If only I can find the right path,
this chain of fear will be cut in half.
Tomorrow, back ramrod-straight,
I will carry her through that gate.
My eyes must be bright
and show no fear.
That big road to freedom,
Is very near here?

A Vocation

'Nurse, Nurse!' Oh, not you again,
my arms and feet won't stand that strain.
The back is numb, the head is hot
such they say is a nurse's lot.

Eight long hours I've been here today,
a few more to go before rest and play.
Make the beds, wash sick hands,
daydreaming of a handsome man.

This is not like the movies,
picture this if you can,
I am not an angel with a halo
just a washer of bed pans.

My mother is proud,
to all she does boast,
'My daughter has a vocation,
that's better than most!'

Oh, Mother dear, it's 1969,
the idea of vocation is out of line!
Back-breaking work, to be sure,
no, Mother, I can't take anymore.

'Nurse, Nurse!' Yes, I am here,
I look at your face and wipe the tears.
Do not be afraid, soon it will be better,
take this medicine, I'm sorry it's bitter.

As I smooth the pillow, you smile at me,
maybe it's worth it, I'll wait and see.
A vocation, Mother, I don't think so
however, that smile will make me have a go!

Dancing On Moonbeams

My childhood was filled with stories,
read to me each day,
rabbits, bears, princesses
all came along the way.
But my favourite tale
my grandmother told,
about a dancing girl
pretty and bold.
Ghosts and bogeymen
she laughed at,
'Why?' you may say,
because she was waiting
for the moonbeams
to carry her heart away.

Grass beneath her feet,
tingled as she danced,
her arms opened wide
to catch the moonbeams.
Dainty pointed toes,
led her round and round,
in a trance-like manner
never uttering a sound.
Whatever band played
the music in her head,
it beat a steady rhythm,
touching the moonbeams
that kissed her feet with freedom.

Goodbye Grandma

The funeral is over, consoling words said
a life gone, our acceptance of its death.
Then reality, there is still more to do
who can fill my grandma's shoes?
Her house so still, cold, somehow,
yet, warm sun is flickering,
over there; through the boughs.
The swing she pushed me on
is still strong, her birds at the table,
look up and burst into song.
I pack up her clothes, clean and pressed,
maybe they will help someone in distress.
Old-fashioned aprons, pink twin-sets,
buttons in place, of course the best dress.

In the bottom drawer, joy beyond measure,
many things that Grandma so treasured.
A letter to Santa, written by my mum,
childish writing, she wanted a drum.
An embroidered hankie, stitches in blue,
a mat of French knitting, I made this too.
Letters from Grandpa while he was at war
photographs, cards, ornaments galore.
Bits of tat that had no price
not to anyone but Grandma,
how comforting, how nice.
Stay in my heart, always be near,
but goodbye for now,
time to wipe my tears.

Lover Of Mine

I can remember, all those years ago
you said you adored me and would never let me go.
It will never last, the sceptics declare
his passive nature and her fiery hair.

Forty years on, yes, the fire has faded
your passiveness has rubbed off on me
but now I am contented.

I see a shiny head, unseen hands put on my shoe,
deep brown eyes look up to mine
twinkling as they do.

I hold your face and kiss it,
oh yes, there is still fire within.
up come your arms, you hold me
I feel your adoration start to cling.

Look back my darling lover
those sceptics have long gone.
Visiting divorce courts, adoration and fire is quashed,
those in a hurry to condemn us have well and truly lost!

A Life Worth Living

Water in the eyeline reaching to the clouds
fingertips of the white crested waves reach out
before pointing back towards the shore,
such a lovely sight, so fresh, so pure.
However, watch yourself my darling
be not complacent or cocksure,
for this blue beauty hides a fierce demeanour
it may suck you down; it may make you whimper.

The whispering breeze is carrying a mournful voice,
cooing peacefully like a dove.
Will it lure you to the water,
can it crush your sense of reason?
Breathe in that fresh ozone then look at the crested waves,
can you see the scales of the mermaids' tails?
Are they playing hide and seek with you,
or just offering an easy way to deep sleep?

Will you choke on that saltwater
as it floods into your soul?
Will you rethink your life again,
maybe want it all retold?
Can you remember the old fisherman's story
how sailors were led to their death?
They followed these lovely visions
whose song promised tranquillity and rest.

You know, reality is just a choice
fight on, or give in and start a rapid decline.
Is life really that pointless
so dull and oh, so benign?
Do you really see life as all pain,
look closer, there is sunshine somewhere.
Rub your eyes, you may see a rainbow
Then hear the warmth of a kind word.

The mermaids may laugh as you go under
blue waves will swell on your self-pity,
they put no value on what your life offers,
just another salty soul to float in their coffins.
Someone, somewhere, may need your love
offer it with kindness as others do.
You could try; your life does have value
maybe you cannot see it, maybe they do.

Still Searching

For fifty-odd years I've been looking for me,
an impossible task it has proved to be.
I have no time to sit and dream,
when I do, the telephone rings!
Another request is made, or a tale of woe,
'You cope so well,' little do they know!

My insides scream, 'I don't want to try,
not today, maybe never,' I want to cry.
Time for me to find my dreams,
to write a book, to plot and scheme.
I would miss you all but for just a while,
give me space and I'll return with a smile.

If I found me, just who would I be,
an explorer, an author, a cherry tree?
Anybody, anything, really would do,
surely, this reflection will not come too!
Where has the person inside me gone?
maybe this will be my eternal song.

I am determined to find her,
she who is me,
Or, should I say who I want to be?
I do not want to miss,
All I think I have missed,
in the years spent looking for me.

Love's Lament

As the post drops to the floor
I am dreaming of a man I adore.
Are all these cards just from him?
Dear Saint Valentine, do not be dim!
Make him think of me today
I am ready for the love game to play.

Cards whose verses were chosen with care
do you think he is aware,
Of how my heart is all a'flutter?
Now my words start to stutter!
Just the thought of his dear face,
please give me a chance to fall from grace.

I put the envelopes on the table,
then sit and contemplate my navel.
Have I the courage to look at the writing,
Is there something here that is exciting?
Who wrote this? Oh what bliss!
was this envelope sealed with a kiss?

I have no idea who it is from
however, let's find out where my heart belongs.
I will put the others in the bin
no one then will read my sin.
My own handwriting in disguise
well, I have to uphold my pride!

Now on my mantle, there it sits
sealed by someone else's lips.
Thank you, thank you, Saint Valentine
someone is offering to be mine.
Will I accept? Damn right I will,
loving words just fit my bill.

Me, Waste Time?

I have so many time-wasters
they keep filling up my day,
afternoon films need to be watched
Grandchildren need to play.

No time to shop as my mother did,
despite long opening hours.
For me no fast-food takeaways
thank goodness for the microwave!

My home is full of gadgets,
all designed to save some time.
The Internet is my latest toy,
but the house is full of grime.

These things provide no elbow grease
they are not worth a dime,
I spend hours just moaning to myself
'No time, no time, no time.'

I think I will forget it all
there's that new book I bought online,
I can while away an hour
reading hints that save you time.

A War To End Wars?

How many men were led to the slaughter,
leaving behind young sons and daughters?
They thought this was a war to end wars,
did they realise enemies would still knock at the door?
More than eighty years have passed and in that time
many mothers have wept as their sons still die.
Each battle fought, be it large or small
is always a part of a war to end wars.

Weapons and tactics may have changed
however, death is mourned just the same.
Young sons and daughters will miss a father's love
who ordered this bloodbath, whose lord up above?
Whatever you believe in, it is no God's will
but man's desire for blood to spill.

Who has seen the enemy at the door,
not he who is fighting in this war to end wars!
A mother's son, a death spoken of lightly
who proudly fell for King and country.
When November comes, blood reappears
colouring poppies but not shielding tears.
Old soldiers' stories may start to bore
as they remember their war to end wars.

Men in soft slippers, not blood-stained boots
woods full of birdsong not gun-toting troops.
Understanding words, hands in soft gloves
surely, that would please anybody's God above?
A war using words is a long hard fight,
try to pursue it with all your might.
Then fathers will be with the children they adore
moreover, we will have won a war to end wars.

Thomas Mutangiri

I was born on 28th January 1964 in Masvingo South Province, Fort Victoria by then. I am the seventh in a family of eight, six boys and two girls. Born in a rural area in a family of poor background. I did primary education for eight years at Mazani Primary School and went on to do secondary education at Jichidza Missionary School forty miles away during the peak of the Zimbabwe liberation war. I used to travel to the mission school on foot at the beginning and end of every school term with a trunk of my goods on my head since my parents could not afford the bus fare.

The school was finally closed on 15th June 1979 because of the intensity of the war and I was forced to be a liberation war collaborator at such a tender age. Survived two attacks by the Rhodesian Air Force jets by the skin of the teeth.

I write poetry partly as a hobby, and secondly as a way of putting the message across the world that *dictatorship* even on a small scale is not at all good in any society. What really influences me to write is the plight of ordinary people in most African states which is so pathetic regardless of Africa being a *giant* in natural resources. My main aim is to try and tell Africans in particular, 'Let's come of age and work for the future of a better Africa. We might not be the immediate beneficiaries but our great grandchildren will benefit if we work together.' Dictatorship is the *major cause* of the African crisis, not *colonialism* as many portray it. Colonialism brought so many good things to Africa, but don't distort me, I don't support the *oppression* and *segregation* of the *black* majority that was done by the *colonialists.*

Last, but not least, I write about *love.* I strongly believe every man needs a woman to share his heart and vice-versa. You might be a multi-billionaire but without a woman to share that money with, that money is not worth having. I also write about our everyday life.

If Only We Had That Precious Liquid

If only we had that precious liquid, our problems might have been history by now.
If only we had that precious liquid, the *International Community* might have taken our problems seriously.
If only we had that black liquid, most superpowers would have more interest in our crisis.

Alas we don't have, and my poor people are paying heavily for that.
Alas we don't have, and my poor people are killed and maimed by a cruel dictator.
Alas we don't have, our people are deliberately starved by a cruel dictator.
Alas we don't have, our mothers and sisters are gang-raped at will by agents of a merciless dictator.

Hey you, *OPEC,* can't you throw us a *barrel* of this precious liquid and our problems will be solved *overnight*? Who can come to our rescue and we will pay him with our *fertile land*?

I really wish Zimbabwe had *oil!*

The Independence That Never Was

The road was so rocky, dusty and thorny that we walked through on our way to *'freedom'*.
The rivers were wide, deep and full of hungry crocodiles that we crossed on our way to *'freedom'*.
The pain was worth enduring since we want to drive out colonialists who had oppressed us for nearly a century.
The guns were heavy and accurate that were fired against us on our way to *'freedom'*.
The jungles were infested with hungry lions and poisonous snakes that we meandered through on our way to *'freedom'*.

The fighter-bombers were armed with lethal explosives that were dropped on top of our unprotected heads, on our way to *'freedom'*.
On 18th April 1980, our efforts were finally rewarded. We were granted 'independence' by our former colonial master, Britain, after nearly two decades of a bloody and destructive war.

Two decades down the line our so-called freedom is in *tatters*.
We are oppressed by the very same person who claims to be our *liberator*, even harder. We are tortured and murdered for simply one reason, *expressing our views.*
Honestly, if that is what we fought for, then that *so-called independence* is not worth having.

Two decades down the line our mothers and sisters are gang-raped by our *so-called liberators*. Our fathers and brothers are persecuted by our so-called liberators for airing their view. Many have taken refuge in our former colonial master, Britain. They have begged, 'Oh Mother Queen, have mercy on us.'

The merciful Mother Queen has accepted us to be part of the royal family. We are now asylum seekers in our former colonial master, *what a shame.* Our so-called liberators are killing and maiming the people they claim to have liberated.

My Zimbabwe, a country millions of miles away from independence. Zimbabwe - *'the independence'* that never was.

I Wish I Were British

I wish I were British, I would express my views without fear of *persecution*.
I wish I were British, I would demonstrate freely in the streets
when politicians have wronged the voters.
I wish I were British, I would be part and parcel of a *democratic* society.
I wish I were British, I would be part and parcel of a *transparent*
political system.

I wish I were British, I would hear of *dictators* in dreams and the media.
I wish I were British, I would use my vote to choose my leaders.
I wish I were British, I would use the *ballot not the bullet* to
remove incompetent leaders.

Hey you ungrateful Britons consider yourself lucky to live in the
most democratic society on the planet. Oh, how lucky you are,
I wish I were you!

Money Can't Buy Happiness

I thought I was in my own world when he courted me.
I did have a positive answer before he even opened his mouth.
Blood was fast flooding in all my nerves from head to toes with joy.
Six months down the line we were husband and wife with
Bill, the millionaire. It was Heaven before death to me.
We promised 'Death to do us part.'

My own world turned to be my own prison.
My blood was fast clotting in all my nerves from head to toes with
    boredom and sorrow.
It was Hell before death to me.
Not only was he a womaniser, he was an abuser in every sense.
Divorce not death did us part six months after.
One thing I have learnt, money will never buy happiness!

My Abusive Husband

You promised me *love*, *adoration* and *admiration* when we married.
You promised *good reception, good respect* and *good romance*.
I thought I was going to be the happiest person when I put the wedding
ring round your finger, alas, I was wrong.

My *once beautiful* face is like a demolished street of *Baghdad*.
My *once sexy body* is like a *bullet-ridden* body of a wounded soldier.
It's now filled with permanent scars.

You promised me *peace*, *love* and *harmony* when we married.
You promised me to be your *better half* and part of your family.
I thought I was going to be the happiest person when you fathered me,
alas I was wrong.

Not only did you *kick* and *headbutt* me like a soccer ball, you even beat
me with clenched fists when I was pregnant with your child.
Not only did you *accuse* me of cheating on you though you are the
one who destroyed my *virginity* and made me pregnant, you even
abandoned your child before he was even born.

My abusive husband, I don't want to *see* you in my life again.

Let's Not Forget Our Hero

Do you still remember the days of *slavery*, when most Black Africans were forced to work for nothing around the globe?

Many were separated from their loved ones and never reunited. Many will never know their blood relatives.
They were forced to work in the sugar and coffee plantations in the Americas. Others were forced to work in the industrial sector in the developing Europe.

Freedom for them was a mere *dream*. Only one man made an end to this cruelty. A man whose statue should be standing in every African street as a mark of respect.

William Wilberforce, the great man who finally ended slavery in Britain in 1833. His influence made the world at large, abandon this evil system.

Abraham Lincoln followed in his footsteps and stopped slavery in the Americas in 1863.

Africa, Africa, let's not forget our fallen hero.
A *'Wilberforce Day'* is a 'must' on our continent.

What Kind Of People Are We?

Africa, what kind of people are we?
Think of the Mozambique floods 2000
The first planes to come to our brothers' rescue were from Europe,
30,000 miles away, *quite amazing*. Where were *we* when we were
needed most?
Where were you Zimbabwe when your long-time ally was giving birth
on a flooded *treetop*? You were too busy fondling with the boobs of
your girlfriend in the comfort of your bed, when your neighbour five
minutes away, was crying 'Help!'

Where were you Zambia, Malawi and Tanzania when you were
needed most? You were busy organising with your *rhino poachers*
which game parks to poach where game wardens were off duty.

Where were you Botswana and Namibia when you were needed most?
You were busy watching porn videos in the comfort of your homes
when your neighbour a few miles away was crying, 'Help!'

Where were you, our *giant* South Africa when you were needed most?
You decided to go after finishing a cup of tea.
Think of the *Rwanda genocide* when crocodiles complained of too
much *human flesh in their rivers.* The *Sierra Leone* crisis when
vultures had a field day on *human corpses in the streets of Freetown.*
When Europe and America intervened we accused them of *double
standards.*

Let's peel off this *selfishness and self-centred scale* once and for all.
Let's come off the *non-considerate cocoon* forever.

Africa, what kind of people are we?

Let's Stop The Bug

If dogs and cats can forgive each other, why can't Tom and Dick forgive one another?
If the ducks and chickens can share the same *trough* why can't *Tracey* and *Trisha* share the same plate?

If donkeys and horses can share the same *stable*, why can't *Jimmy* and *John* share the same house.
If *lions* and *hyenas* can't fight in the jungle, why did *George* and *Saddam* fight in the *Gulf?*

If the strong *Berlin Wall* has fallen down, why can't this *colour wall* fall as well?

Hey you *uncivilised* people, *black, white, pink* or *red,* let's stop this *racist bug* and live together peacefully as human beings.
Let's make this world a *multi-racial* environment.

Whose Fault Is It?

'Sorry my friend, I kicked you yesterday, it wasn't my fault, the
problem was I was under the influence of alcohol.'
'It's OK, pal, it's over.'

'Sorry my darling, I had a one-night stand yesterday, the *problem* was,
I had taken too many drugs.'
'Never mind, honey, I will forgive and forget.'

'Sorry Mum I called you names yesterday, the *problem* was I had
taken too many glasses of lager at the club.'
'Never mind, I still love you my son.'

'Sorry pal I couldn't pay back the money you lent me, it wasn't my
fault, the *problem* was I was serving a three-month jail term for
drunken driving.'
'Never mind, we are still friends and forget about paying back,
let's focus on the future.'

Did the *drugs* force their way into your nerves?
Did the *alcohol* force its way through your mouth to your tummy,
or did you?
Did the *lager* force its way into your nerves to the brain or did you?
Did the *jail* ever knock at your door and invite you into one of its cells?
If not, whose fault is it?

Let's Find A Cure

Africa, Africa, let's put our *act* together and find a cure for our *dependent syndrome.* Let's find a lasting solution to our problems. Crying unfair Europe or America will never bring food to our tables. Our *dependent syndrome* must be cured once and for all.

Africa, Africa, let's put our *act* together and stop the rot. Let's stop biting the very hand that is feeding us. Let's not forget the billions of dollars and material aid these American and European donors are pouring into Africa. What are we giving in return? *Nothing!*

Africa, Africa, let's find a *cure* for our *dependent syndrome as a matter of urgency.*

Africa, Africa, let's not always cry *'Unfair western trade, unfair western trade.'* Can't we *trade* amongst ourselves? Let's not always cry *'Racist west racist west.' Racism* is everywhere but unfortunately Africa has nowhere to practise it since they depend entirely on these so-called *racists* for survival.

Africa, Africa, let's *come of age* and build a foundation for our future generation. Europe was not like this fifty years ago, they put their *act* together and put Europe on the map.

Africa, Africa, let's put our *act* together and put Africa on the map like the rest of the world has done.

Africa, Africa, let's find a *cure* for the *dependent syndrome* as *a matter of urgency* or we will die a *laughing stock.*

My Sugar Mummy

Come on my sugar 'sixty-six' show me age is nothing but simply a number.
Show me you are a body language *technician*.
Cling to me like a limpet, entwine me like a liana with your lovely arms.
Show me the twenty-seven-year gap between us is simply a number.
My sugar mummy, at sixty-six she only looks twenty.

Come on my sugar sixty-six, show me age is nothing but a number.
Flash me your hefty butterfly-tattooed boobs, quench my thirst
with your *steaming love* and mop my *tears of joy* with a lovely kiss.
My sugar mummy, at sixty-six she only looks twenty.

Come on my sugar sixty-six, show me that the big gap between us
is nothing but a number.
On the *comfort* of our *double bed* you are a star, even the long nights
of winter become short.
Oh, my *sexual healer*, what a lucky man I am.
My sugar mummy at sixty-six she only looks twenty.

My sugar mummy, like *wine and whisky*, she gets better with age.
Oh my sugar sixty-six, bandage my body with your soft arms and
make me happy.
My sugar mummy, it's now time for bed.

Can't You Hear The Voice In The Gutter

As the hope of a quick solution to our crisis is slowly but surely melting away, my emotions are growing bigger and more uncontrollable by the day. As the minds of the *International Community* are slowly but surely giving their backs to the suffering masses, the merciless *dictator* is having a field day and boasting himself *'the untouchable'*.

As the once green forests of our once lovely country are slowly but surely becoming a *desert* because of uncontrolled cutting of trees, my emotions are growing bigger and bigger by the day. As our once *bread basket* of Africa is now becoming a *bread beggar* of Africa, my emotions explode like atomic bombs.

As the reality of total *neglect* by the international world is slowly but surely clotting my circulatory system, that pain is getting the better of me. Even our own neighbours are spitting at us like stinking corpses, when we cry 'Help.' Whenever I get on line to talk with family and friends back home, I always hear words of *sorrow* and *suffering*. My own people are dying a slow but surely painful death. They are either starved, killed or raped for not supporting the ruling *despot!*

The *AIDS carnage* is not sparing them either. *Three thousand AIDS corpses* are buried every week . The cost of living is beyond their reach, the cost of dying is beyond their reach as well because they can't afford the costs to bury the dead.

Where should my people go? They can't afford *life* and they can't afford *death*. The International Community, can't you *hear* that *voice* in the *gutter?* Zimbabwe needs your *attention!*

Margaret Ginz

Margaret was born in London, the third of four daughters. She always had a great interest in the countryside and natural history. In 1940 she joined the Women's Land Army and drove a Fordson tractor for ploughing. She milked cows and reared pigs and chickens.

Her best subject at school was English and she started to write poetry and stories at a very young age.

Margaret has always had a great love of animals and lives in Cambridge with her pet cat, Sheba.

Her first poem to be published was called 'Midsummer Night' which was published in 2003 by the BBC Eastern Counties, in a volume of listeners' poems called 'Your Poems!'

Margaret has a married daughter who lives in a Hertfordshire village, and a son who is a restaurateur in Cambridge.

Her hobbies are writing and music and at present she is learning to play the violin.

The Snowdrop

When spring comes late, the flowers wait
To don their fancy frocks.
The message goes from bud to bud
From quince to scented phlox.

The harebell tells the daffodil
The tulip tells the rose
And tender leaves stay tightly curled
Until each blossom knows,

It is not time to venture forth
The wind is blowing cold
But one small rebel does not heed
She's tough and she is bold.

She dons her fairy cloak of white
And pushes from below.
She pushes up with all her might
Through frosty earth and snow.

This is the essence of delight,
Sweet harbinger of spring.
It is the snowdrop, pearly-white
That causes hearts to sing.

Nightfall

The Earth now dons her cloak of grey
To end the shining summer's day.
The sun sets golden in the west,
This is the time of sleep and rest.

Yet with the coming of the night,
Whilst creatures slumber, others might
Come suddenly to life as they
In daylight have to hide away.

So now sleep on, you rustic squire,
Sleep like the cattle in your byre.
Just dream your dream of love and lust
And let those stay awake who must.

For life goes on from dusk till dawn
And though you wake up in the morn
Some creatures hurry to their rest
To sleep till sun sets in the west.

Spring Harmony

The air is full of music now,
The buds are fresh and green.
New life is bursting from each bough,
It is a magic scene.

This is the time of hope reborn,
Of friendship, joy and love,
Of gentle sunlight shining down
When skylarks sing above.

Now sings the music of the year,
The opera of the dawn.
The greys of winter disappear,
White blossom on the thorn.

Just feel the lifeblood stirring
In meadow, wood and lea.
Come see the rustic ballet now
For spring is on its way.

Wings

Strong wings beating, lifting, turning
Ever upward through the air.
Floating, gliding, ever yearning
Dappled gold in sunlit glare.
Soft wings shining, ever envied
By the ones who, full of care,
Long to fly from troubled waters
And, like birds, the sky to share.
Strong wings beating, lifting, turning
Ever upward through the air.

Wild Horses

The horses come galloping over the hill,
Galloping over the hedgerow and rill.
Fire in the belly and fire in the eye
Flecks of white foam floating up to the sky.
Galloping, galloping, thundering past
Tail flicking upward and outward so fast.
Steam from smooth flanks rising into the air,
Galloping onwards with never a care.
Galloping, galloping, mile upon mile
Over brushwood and hillock, gateway and stile.
Thundering, plundering all in their way
Galloping on to the end of the day.

The Mousling

A tiny mousling scurries by
With flicking tail and flashing eye.
He never even questions why
Huge creatures from him shy.

He knows not of his destiny
He only knows that he must flee
From anything that he might see
As big as you and me.

The Storm

We sat upon the swinging branch
Sweet Dorothy and I.
We savoured every moment
And we could not say goodbye.

We knew the night was drawing near
And daylight growing dim.
The lonely forest drew no fear,
We had our swinging limb.

We sat upon it cosily
So cosy and so warm.
We loved our sturdy oak tree
And did not foresee the storm.

It came upon us suddenly
With blazing mad affray.
The icy shafts of rain came down
To drench all in its way.

The thunder was horrendous.
The lightning lit the sky.
Oh how we clung together then
Sweet Dorothy and I.

A sudden crack, then all went black
And lightning struck the tree.
Then we were flung into the air
Sweet Dorothy and me.

Three days before they found her,
My Dorothy Malone.
The lonely forest claimed her
To be its very own.

Our lovely tree is ruined now
The swinging limb has gone
But under black and twisted bough
My Dorothy lives on.

She bides in peaceful wooded glade
With primrose, fern and moss.
I sit with her in dappled shade
And ponder on my loss.

On moonlit nights I wander there
I wander there alone.
Sometimes I see the swinging limb
And Dorothy Malone!

The Sparrows In My Garden

The sparrows in my garden
Are a joyous sight to see,
They vie for places on the fence
And crowd the rowan tree.

They fight and chirp and quarrel
Like a host of noisy tots,
They peck and scratch the soft brown earth
And dance round flower pots.

They never seem to worry
When the tabby cat strolls by
And when she stops and stares at them
They never blink an eye.

They shout out for their breakfast,
It must be there by eight.
I feel extremely guilty
If ever I am late.

So I am never lonely
They are always there to see.
With the sparrows in my garden
We are one big family.

A Christmas Wish

'Please how much is a robin?'
Said the curly-headed tot.
'I think I'd like to buy one
With some money that I've got.

We never had a real one
Just a wooden one you see
Each Christmastime we get him out
And sit him in the tree.

So, how much is a robin please?
I'm quite prepared to pay
Then Christmastime I'll get him out
And watch him fly away!'

The Bluebell Wood

I lingered in a bluebell wood
And wondered if indeed I should.
It seemed the wood belonged to them
Of perfect flower and leaf and stem.

And then I bent more close to see
A most delightful symmetry
Of wondrous deep and azure blue
And naturally compounded hue.

My cares all seemed to fade away.
Oh would that I could stay all day.
Such heavenly place, this realm of peace
To which is given so short a lease.

I had to leave this place so rare.
Now in that woodland all is bare.
But in my heart, the bluebells stay
To live forever and a day.

Winter

With dignity the garden dies
Gone are the flowers and bees
The children run with sparkling eyes
A small sharp wind blows fallen leaves.

The hoar frost on the cherry bough
Reflects a rosy glow
Of Phoebus rising in the east
To warm the earth below.

Stark filigree of leafless tree
Shows dark against the light
And in the deep and icy sky
A crescent moon hangs bright.

The frozen earth is dormant now
And morning skies are grey.
But buds are on the apple bough
Can spring be far away?

Midsummer Night

Now silently the moonlight steals
Across the shimmering lawn.
The fragrant blossoms curl in sleep
Until the early morn,
The dew falls gently on the fern
An owl gives plaintive cry
Small pearly nestlings snuggle close
And dream that they can fly.

A tiny rustle issues forth
From heap of fallen leaves.
Small beady eyes peep out
Soft whiskers tremble in the breeze.
The silver-throated nightingale
Holds stage in rowan tree.
A blackbird joins in chorus
To protect his territory.

Sure-footed toad leaps silently
On unsuspecting prey.
A golden snail leaves silver trail
And wends a tedious way
Along the footpath, so to reach
Her nest by break of day.
Then all is still, beyond the hill
Comes silvery light of dawn.
And Phoebus rising greets the world -
A brand new day is born.

To A Blackbird

Sweet blackbird in the willow tree,
Why do you sit and sing?
Is it that your gladness shows - or do you feel faint brush of fear,
That your dear nestlings may not know
The ecstasy of being here?

Whilst frantically you build your nest,
Do you not wonder why?
Rough winds will shake the fragile bough, on which your efforts lie.
In time for nature's duplicate,
You work unceasing, without rest, to build the perfect habitat.
Sweet blackbird - tell me why?

Mother's Day Or (The Mix-Up)

Last Mother's Day, I thought that I would have a quiet day.
The year before, my children both, had let it slip away -
     without remembering.
Not their fault, I told myself, they have such busy lives.
They owe me nothing after all - imagine my surprise -
When at the door at half-past nine, there stood a handsome boy,
His arms were full of blooms, his face just beamed with purest joy.
'I hope you have a lovely day,' he said, then drove away.
The card said, 'Lots of love to you, and Happy Mother's Day!'

My house transformed was fragrant with those blossoms bright and sweet
I rearranged them once again, and then just by my feet -
A piece of paper floated down, and on it in clear view -
The number of the house stood out and it said 'number two'!
Now I was in a pretty state - the bouquet all undone -
I'd got to wrap it up again - I live at number one!
The cellophane was in the bin - the ribbon all in tatters.
Whatever am I going to do? I wonder if it matters?
Shall I just take them as they are, arranged in jugs of water? -
Or just keep quiet - pretend they're mine!
I really shouldn't oughta!

As I stood cogitating thus - the doorknocker went bang!
There stood the smiling youth once more -
'Another for you Ma'am!'
This time it really was for me, and all I had to do,
Was change the label stuck on there from 'one' to 'number two'.
We both enjoyed our 'Mother's Day', I never had to tell!
I had her flowers - she had mine - it all went rather well.
Next time I'll read the label first, because it's understood -
The flowers our children send to us - are priceless - and so good.

Steven James Long

Born in 1979, I am now 24 years old. However, it seems to me that I have experienced a lifetime of emotion already.

I have been writing poetry from an early age and have always enjoyed the creative experience of putting pen to paper.

Having spoken to a few other poets it seems from their observations that the way I write is unusual. By this I mean that where other writers may ponder their subject matter, and spend hours, sometimes days, returning to their work to refine it, I, on the other hand, though I am sure it is not unique, spend no more than 2/3 minutes on any verse. Whether they are long or short, my poems are always put down in a very rapid fashion. I find this a very natural and flowing way to write. I also find that without thought and instinctive writing, my poetry retains a kind of rawness. Of this, I am particularly thankful as it means I can always recall the emotions at the time of writing.

My style of writing is always rhyming verse. Of this, I feel a little limited in style, although others say they find it difficult to write rhyming verse. Therefore, I suppose it depends on your point of view whether it is a gift or a curse.

The main influences to all my poems are my life experiences. These are mainly focussed on love, loss, passion and nature.

I write poetry purely for my own enjoyment. As some may keep photograph albums, I keep my poems as a reminder of my life. Recently though, having built up a large body of work over many years, I would like to turn my passion into a career.

Greed

Cosmetic surgeons
Increasing their wealth
Who won't take a pay cut
For the 'every man's' health

Corrupted and selfish
For personal gain
Heartless black souls
Uncaring and vain

There was once faith in humanity
During struggles and hardship
Now it saddens the heart
That it's money we worship.

True Love

Gentle touch of trembling hand
Two naked hearts that understand
That true passion of flesh requires a trust
An emotional bond beyond the boundaries of lust
As you lie together in sensual depth
The world stops around you as if it's bereft
Of the turn of its axle and time set in stone
Two souls become one, no longer alone.

Farewell Jo

I so wept once you'd gone
Burning tears stung my eyes
My heart still so fragile
Cut down by surprise

No more love left to give me
No more tears left to cry
My soul weeps for you gently
And my heart says 'Goodbye.'

Life's Walk

May we walk through this life
Hand in hand, side by side
Being there for each other
Enjoying the ride

May our paths never stray
Let us both walk together
From moonlight till sunrise
Together, forever

Our bond is so special
It is pure and it's true
And if the walk we share's hard
Then I'll carry you!

Inspiration

O' wondering thought
That wonders the mind
O' wondering thought
Be you gentle and kind

O' wondering thought
So frequent and sure
O' wondering thought
Be you simple and pure

O' wondering thought
That pulses the heart
O' wondering thought
You've been there from the start

O' wondering thought
Inspirationally giving
O' wondering thought
You're my reason for living

Beautiful Daydreams

Oh star in the heavens
Such a beautiful sight
When my world is in darkness
You are my shining light

How I want to be with you
Not a moment too soon
Are you over the rainbow
Or just past the moon?

Knowing I'll never reach you
Makes me break down and cry
As you vanish with daybreak
My heart says goodbye.

Magic Sky

Rolling mist on emerald vale
Winter's moon so soft and pale
Yonder high a beautiful star
A traveller's beacon to be seen from afar

A vibrant guide for wandering heart
To lead to another and ne'er be apart
To cast down euphoric and radiant love
Held in wonder and awe that star up above.

Ride The Rainbow

Sleepwalking through life
On a tightrope so thin
Catching lifts on the clouds
Before the rainstorm sets in

Weather the storm
Before the storm weathers you
Steer clear of the grey clouds
Seek the comfort in blue

Take a ride on the rainbow
Let the light be your guide
And you won't be alone
I'll be there by your side.

Love Of An Angel

Angels dance on silver clouds
Their voices sweet with tune
As twinkling stars play symphonies
The sun dances with the moon

Cascading lights that catch your eyes
Reflect the deepest love
Then I know I've found my kindred soul
As it's written up above.

To Mend A Broken Heart

Tears of glass that cut the face
That shred your emotional core
An empty heart that can't replace
The love that it once bore

Fond memories of times gone past
Dissolve into the mists
A love now dormant but meant to last
May be rekindled by true love's kiss

Black Days

The blackest rainbow with colourless rays
The sleepless nights and endless days
A love so deep, eternally lost
Life must go on but what will it cost?

You rule my subconscious
And live in my dreams
When life seems so perfect
It's not what it seems

A love so complete
Filled my heart and my soul
You were the piece of the jigsaw
That made my life whole

Memories fade
But true love remains
You're the beat of my heart
The blood in my veins

The love was so strong
When it broke I did too
I went from being so high
To being so blue

The world seems so cruel
But I still live in hope
The past was so painful
But you helped me to cope

The distance between us
Is as far as can be
Though true love can't be parted
For you and for me.

Rage

The inferno is blazing
A fiery rage
The untamed demon
Set free from his cage

Destruction and terror
Lay wake in his trail
He has no emotion
And preys on the frail

His burning black coals
Scorch through to the heart
As he takes all the love
Then tears it apart

There is no redemption
For the beast's lost his soul
And where once was his heart
There's a smouldering hole.

What Is Love

There is no equation
No numerical form
It is both tranquil and calm
Yet a fiery storm

Not yet conquered by science
Neither mapped out like land
We know not where it comes from
And cannot be planned

You cannot market a product
With such sparkle and fizz
As at the end of the day
Who knows what love is?

Till We Meet Again

What becomes of us?
Where do we go?
Who is to say?
Who is to know?

An eternal slumber?
A dream sugar-sweet?
Where the use of your wings
Is more important than feet

Where the light is pure white
Where no harm can be done
Just past the rainbow
Past the blaze of the sun

If this is where we go
If this is where we stay
Then I'll hopefully find you
Somehow, someday.

Jackie Jones-Cahill

I am a mother of five children and grandmother to three children. I started writing after doing a poem in my family literacy class. Sadly both my parents died within seven months of each other. My mother was the first to leave us and my cousin Maria suggested that I try and write some poetry; she said if I could do this it may help with some of the grief I was carrying. I did not really talk to anyone about my parents' deaths as it was so painful but writing these poems has helped me to cope and go from strength to strength.

Recently I was accepted for a Spotlight Poets' book called 'The Gift Of Perception'.

Approximately fourteen anthologies are to feature my poetry, not bad for one who did not like poetry at school, so to all the people who say, 'Oh, poetry, I don't really like it,' try it! It was amazing to see my work in print for the first time!

I was asked to attend bullying assemblies at the school my children attend, and partake of discussions and read my poetry to a hall full of children. When I had finished my readings, the hall burst into a stamping of feet and hand clapping! I was amazed at this reception and appreciation. Since then I have spoken at a number of meetings, sharing both views and opinions. My poems are now on display in the school along with poetry written by the children, both encouraging the children to talk of a very much otherwise hidden factor, and to write about their 'otherwise not talked about' true feelings. Too many children are feeling that they cannot talk about bullying, some see it as, believe it or not, a weakness to tell tales!

At the moment I am looking forward to having a children's book published, which I have just finished working on.

If my writing has helped just one person, then that will make me the happiest person alive. I hope you enjoy the collection of poetry here; it is based on the truth of life.

Losing You Both

(In memory of my parents Ann Cahill Regan and Gerald Regan)

I still cannot get over losing you both,
This pain is unbearable but what can I do?
I am so sad that I cannot see, feel or hug either of you,
You were both my parents and I miss you.

Never Knew

(Dedicated to my cousin and best friend Maria Ann Cahill)

I never knew I had another cousin,
I had always felt someone was missing.
Don't ask me how, I just did,
Maria searched for her family for twenty-two years,
She must have cried so many tears,
How sad it was, when at the end of her search,
Her mother had died,
Sometimes I wonder how she handled such pain,
She tries to be strong,
But her pain will always be there,
I know I will always be there to show her I truly care.

Told

I was told you were no good for me,
How did they all know and not me?
They could see straight through him,
But they do say love is blind,
I just thought most people were being unkind,
I thought that they were wasting my time.

Now it turns out that they were right,
So I have finished with him,
And ended my plight,
Now, my whole world seems so bright,
I can see such wonderful daylight.

Seventeen

(Dedicated to my ex-husband Michael and my daughter Angie)

I became a mother at seventeen,
I gave birth to the most wonderful daughter you have ever seen,
She weighed seven pounds two and a half ounces at her birth,
All the pain and agony, it was worth,
Her father couldn't believe his eyes and he cried,
He said, 'You have given me a wonderful baby daughter,
My wonderful bride, my wife, my pride!'

Drops Of Rain

Don't just stand there and look at me,
I want everyone to be happy,
If I don't look the same,
It is not my fault, I am not to blame,
Just because I am disabled,
You know, we really are all the same!
I still feel pain,
But I have lots to gain,
I, too, feel the drops of rain,
As I am taken out in my wheelchair.

Mars

I thought the sun would shine so bright,
Even when it was daylight,
I look at the stars,
Will I see Mars
Or do you think that's too far?
Well, I cannot get there in a car!

What If?

What if the clouds were made of pure white snow?
Should we stay or should we go?
If we went, where would we go?
To Heaven and back, who could say so?
Will it be hot? I don't know.
I bet the clouds are fluffy, just like snow.

Wrapped

I looked at the babies in angels' arms,
They will not come to any harm,
I look at my four little ones,
Blue eyes and hair, baby-fair,
I pray they will know I care,
They are waiting till I get there,
Where my heart and soul will to them bare.

Shush!

(In memory of my parents Ann Cahill Regan and Gerald Regan)

My mother and father say 'Shush, shush.
Do not cry, dry your eyes,
We are only up in the sky,
We are sorry we had to die,
It was our time, you see, that is why,
But we will always love you,
We will watch over you.
We are sorry we died.'

Side To Side

Why do you drink and drive?
Does it give you courage inside?
Don't you know you are swerving side to side?
You have just hit somebody, they could die,
You did not even pull over to the side,
You must have known what you had done.
How can you still want to run?
You will see the damage on your car,
As you get out and go in your door,
Have you any conscience?
If not, I can't say anymore,
But think of the person lying on the floor.

Food For The Baby

Why do you want to take drugs?
I know you say it gives you a buzz,
You always seem to be in a rush,
You have been to work and gotten all your wages,
Then I find that you are lying in the daisies,
Money spent for your high,
Did you forget the people you love
And the food for your baby?
You hand me fifty pence,
That is not enough!
I hope your drugs were worth it,
Giving up the family, you say, you loved.

Man And Wife

(Dedicated to Michael)

I've thought about you all my life,
It is so sad we are no longer man and wife,
We were together only two years,
You broke my heart,
I cried so many tears,
All these years, now later passed,
We are talking now at last,
We have grown, forgotten the past.

David Pooley

I was born in Chorley, Lancashire in 1942. I am a family man with children and grandchildren.

On reflection I am extremely lucky to be a written contributor to any anthology, since at the age of nine I was paralysed completely with poliomyelitis. Only the skilled dedication of medical staff and parental devotion prompted my miraculous recovery.

Years later, having left school at the age of sixteen, I worked on my father's farm in Heskin. This I did until the age of twenty-three.

Following my marriage to Lillian in 1965 I sought employment elsewhere since there was work substantially better paid than farmwork. In 1974 we emigrated to South Africa and I worked in ISCOR steelworks returning in 1977 owing to a family bereavement. Repatriation at that time was reluctantly thought best.

Looking ahead my main motivation is to write just one simplified successful poem that will grant immortality long after my spiritual endeavours cease to be.

Lord Byron, Emily Dickinson, and Robert Frost ('Stopping by Woods on a Snowy Evening') are poets that motivate me. William Wordsworth's 'Lucy' and 'Daffodils' are simplicity at their greatest yet so few, including myself, despite constantly striving, could never, or possibly ever, hope to achieve that one lasting feat.

Fly fishing is the outdoor sport I enjoy most as a hobby, but don't go often now due to the rising cost. I enjoy golf occasionally, too.

Still, I like nothing better than my own peaceful solitude outdoors in the country air, always with pencil and notebook, searching for that simple elusive poem of lasting greatness that must arrive: I have far to go!

Michael James

We loved him more than life itself; he knew it with his sigh.
When by his side we cherished, a day, each week, a month.
Resemblance of a brother too; contented not to cry!
Four months on the heartache, frustration, as to why?

Activated on by need, we put full trust in them.
Precious time went wasted by; weeks with little done!
Inconclusive far too long, gifted minds erased of light:
Lost without salvation; assumptions wrong, not right.

Too soon to hear we understand where they cannot comprehend.
Lost on words, an empty hole, a shell-shocked shattered soul.
'Live forever' the sad man said: does he know how true the words?
Although you've gone to Heaven, you're rooted in our hearts.

To rest beside you some day, is fact, not fiction, now.
We will not leave you all alone, hearts not made of stone.
We shall not hear the chatter of birds to hop our way
Nor feel the slightest patter, should squirrels pause to play.

Lady Friend

The liaison not adulterous; no other women, why?
No other lady could beguile; then pleased, look one in the eye.
As friend or foe we didn't know! Her litter unperceived.
Three months on, perception: a treasure disbelieved.

No smell of perfume lingers while sweet words serenade.
Words don't pass as discord, that frowns beneath an eye.
A love that harbours no romance; yet leaves no risk to chance.
That swells one's heart to the brim, and satisfies the soul.

Her loyalty unquestioned; no path down which she'd stray.
No clothes of dress adorn her; yet coat of blue and tan.
A Yorkie true called Suzy, nicknamed 'Lady Friend'.
Someone really special; never far away.

Farmhouse Lament

Alone today as yesterday since someone gave it birth,
A stone-clad aged reminder of human evolution.
Three centuries living off the land; each heavy task to hand.
Cultivating meagre crops: in soil, with too much sand.
Three hundred years upon that land has taken numbered toll.
Every muscle rippled, on limbs it hadn't crippled.
The latest one to pass away had, by far, the longest stay.
Still stood there as yesterday, the old farmhouse today.

Captivation

Active eye done searching: beauty to behold!
Hypnotic to an easy move; the spark ignites a fuse.
Heart now weakly flutters; no weakness there to yield!
Mind becomes besotted; attention centres one.
Mental pictures magnify; torch betrays a beam.
That you become reality: now supersedes the dream.

Regretful Tree

When I lay silent; seen no more,
Cast no shadow by your door.
Think of me, what might have been!
Now remnants of a dream.
Pausing now to stoop and stare,
Of aching heart; did you care?
Too late to reach beyond a gaze,
Reflection of one's ways.
Faced with loss: no hope tomorrow!
Hurt was mingled in with sorrow.
Ignorance that came to be.
Destructive of one's tree.

Pike Hike

Driven by a ritual; unease born with the dawn.
Annual has become the trek, of tired limbs and feet.
Hopeful of a rainless day; yet dew-drenched speckled morn.
Alone not many moments when voices crowd to greet.

With too much missed by many, I'm soon alone again.
Steps of stone, hear no moan, passing through dry lips.
Fields of lambs accounted for, I've ewe-linked every chain.
A cooling drink now taken; refreshing tiny sips.

No longer quite alone stand I, when at the very top.
Views around unlimited; trust test for naked eye,
With mind and eye well satisfied; a wasted visit not.
Lured there each Easter: ritual seasoned, why?

Without Love Cause

Heart was once more racing and still within a mile.
The sight before me mill'co the bends, the bridge, the trees.
On wheels of two I'm flying; defying twists of fate.
Late by twenty minutes yet she will not chide the wait.

Without love's cause I might have just, passed the village by.
An eyelid blink of sunray; some of it not seen!
I fell one day beneath its spell; a maiden fair was kissed.
When we became acquainted, a night was seldom missed.

Thirty years later, and countless journeys through,
Time ain't erased the fervour, the magic lingers still.
That time denotes its change is seen in faces strange,
Sprinklings of the old remain, mingling with the new.

Preferential Turn

I prefer my breath of country air, with farming's prosperous hum.
Industrialised pollution contributes to no one's healthy sum.
I prefer a scenic country stroll down spring's recycling groove.
Rather like our seasons; I'm continually on the move.

I prefer the scenic countryside; those daisies and buttercups.
Houses that are drab and grey, aren't in my view at all.
I prefer my lingered look at life, poised on nature's infinite care.
To be outdoors with nature, is the life that I prefer.

Let me be within that distant view, beyond all smoky haze
What I can see within the eye, won't hurt the lungs at all.
Miles from any city noise; of snarling traffic jams.
In a world that's still revolving; yet does it silently.

Let me be away from city life; of people full of strife.
A dreaded queue was nothing new, but is where I now long to be.
A least a mile from no one; but not alone in nature's way.
In a world that's still revolving; yet does so silently.

Moisturising Need

Nothing new was so much blue, until rain clouds came to view.
Shrubs and plant life withered; green grasses burned to straw.
Riverbeds now narrow; ducks lingering there, are few.
Tiny streams that hold no bream, await the swell of rain.

Near to me the smell of earth, yet my feet ain't touched the soil.
A cloud has burst its bubble, there's rivulets in the stubble.
It was time we had that stain of moisturising rain.
Relieving farmers of the strain; was it drought, or life again.

Had I time to stare tomorrow, at the progress of today.
Select a plant; one blade of grass, to watch it patiently.
I may just see a stunt of growth; released without a sigh.
It wasn't growing yesterday in land that was too dry.

Perfect Day

Greeted with a ripple rise on waters running deep.
Ducks weigh up the sudden threat; heron splashes off.
Moorhens leave the bank side and into reed beds hide.
Swallows swoop the surface where gnats and midges don't survive.
Fish will cruise below this film, undetected to the eye.
On fields of green, sheep now seen, keeping meadow grasses low.
Tree-rise fills the background; gorse and bracken spreads abound.
This pleasant breeze puts one at ease, cooling down the heat.
Time of no momentum; active float gives hint of sport.
Sunshine through the cloudless blue; for me a perfect day.

Childish Pawn

We gave of love unselfishly; answered every call.
But when it came to values, did we really count at all?
Treated with displeasure; tokens for good measure.
Do we really matter though? We only gifted life.

It's down to childish matter; who cares a broken heart?
We see and hear no laughter, with words that play a part.
Where guidance once was needed; no useful role to play.
When one's life lacks a purpose to contribute a say.

We'll maybe see tomorrow in a brighter shade of light,
But won't it be some sunshine to warm an aching heart?
We will not feel the inner glow, or proudly share a joy.
There as pawns between us now: down to childish ploy.

Loving You

Hard to keep the vacant look; she walked into the room.
Thoughts then lying dormant, flare instantly to life!
Beauty of such splendour, heartbreak kissed away!
Downcast and disheartened with the role to play.
Deep depression far and wide; guilty secrets, much to hide!
Loving you for just one day; daunting task in every way.
For you there's no beginning to justify an end,
For me an end that can't begin to justify the start.
Time and places pushed aside; delusive love to be denied.
Dreams are not reality: facts would soon divide.

Forever Mum

To us you were forever Mum; selfish as that seems.
We never thought you'd want a say; to end another day.
For when the rising of the sun reveals true absence of a mum,
It hits home hard; leaves grave message on a card.

You'll live with me forever, Mum, in sentimental thoughts,
You could not share with everyone, commitment, love or life!
Time may heal a broken heart; maybe ease the pain.
Forever left to ponder: was I not some way to blame?

Not for you the easy life; you had enormous strife!
From life's tree leaf, a book of grief, too much for anyone.
Let's just say you had your way of independent pride,
May love embrace you evermore; at peace the other side.

Dad's Gift

He gave my life true measure; an image I now treasure.
He taught me how to live each day in some respectful way.
Why did I not pay heed, to his much-burdened need?
His need of helping hands from me; was I barely there to see?
How tired he'd become, all work without the fun.
Till haggardly, it was tragically, too late to alter fate.
Time overtakes a healthy soul; the ailing half the span.
I miss him now, a guiding light; his shadow but the grave
For evermore remembered: for the gift of life he gave.

Endless Days

I'm where I'll always want to be; closely by your side.
Encompassed in your arms once more; sweet lady I adore!
Love your hair in natural flair, long or flowing as needs be.
The ponytail that never fails to add more sparkle to your smile.
Those ruby lips, I long to kiss: tilt your head towards moonlight!
See you slowly close your eyes, feel your heartbeat, gentle sighs.
Respect your unpretentious ways; know such beauty's born to stay.
Love you in so many ways - I'm wanting endless days!

Disrespectful Crystals White

Respect those crystals on the ground; white carpet everywhere.
It matters little on stone wall with no climbers there to fall.
Tread like you're in water deep; since in walking sense you are!
Domestic pile of multigrain is safely snug indoors,
Than this one underfoot belies, of painful contact, hurtful cries.
Broken limbs a'plenty; some lovers' beds lie empty.
Sheer madness all around, ignoring glitter on the ground.
Novice climbers had good sense, to stay below a stone-walled fence.
Skaters on thin ice today; should not weight water that wouldn't
    hold a sleigh!
On wheels that go too fast, can be one's journey last.
Bones of brokenness to heal; the dead too numb to feel.
Disrespectful crystals white upon the ground: respect no life or limb.

Rebecca Powell

My name is Rebecca Powell and I am almost twenty-five years old. I have a partner called Craig and we have been together now for seven and a half years. We have two young children who are Brandon and Savannah, aged six and four years.

I grew up in a fairly large family consisting of myself, two sisters and one brother. I left secondary school in 1995 with a handful of GCSE passes and then went on to college where I completed a course in business studies.

I left home at eighteen and moved in with my partner.

I have started various college courses including a media studies course, law, and a photography course, but unfortunately did not complete them.

I write poetry because I love the way that in poetry you can express feelings in any style whatsoever - I have an excellent imagination. I am a dreamer and I am a total optimist. I always try to see the best in people and things around me, and I believe if you set your heart on something and you really believe in yourself then you can achieve anything. I believe that the 'world is your oyster'.

A lot of the inspiration for my poetry comes from my views on life, and the life in which we live. When I look through my work, I see myself, that this is a recurring theme. I find also, that being a mother is a huge inspiration when writing poetry because I find that being a parent brings with it emotions that can only be found from the special bond you can feel with your own children. I also find inspiration from the bond that my partner and I share too.

I am also a huge believer in spiritualism, ghosts and suchlike, and find that I also get a lot of my inspiration from my beliefs in these. A couple of my poems are also dedicated to this.

I have many hobbies and I am very much into holistic therapy, and as well as my dream of becoming a writer, I also hope that very soon my dream of having my own business selling everything spiritually related will materialise. I love very tranquil settings surrounded by trees, streams and lakes, and it is also my dream to one day visit Canada.

Time

So precious is time
It must be grasped and held tight
Hold onto every second
For every second you must fight

For life is so precious
So dear yet so true
So many things to fit in
So much to do

So many things to say
So many things to make right
Always look ahead
Always look for the light

There is so much happiness
If you only do look
So just take one second
Of this such precious time

Take a second to think
You will realise
All the love that surrounds you
All the people that care

The love that was
That will always be there

So take a few more moments
Of this such precious time
To think over your life
Think of times gone past

So many feelings and emotions
Many good times have passed
But the good times have been
Yet still they are there

There are people that love you
There are people who care
So say all those things
That you intended to say

Do not keep them back for another day
For the love between families and friends is for life
It's a bond always there
Grown deep over time

We sometimes need reminding
Reassurance of that love
We can take one another for granted
We may need a little push

But love is so precious
Something to treasure
There may not always be the time
But we must make sure it's known forever

So precious is time
It must be grasped and held tight
Hold onto every moment
For every second we must fight

The Ninth Of November

The sound of the sea
The calm of the air
The feeling of things
You can't see
But are there

The clear blue ocean
The feel of the sand
The warmth that I feel
I feel in my hands

Lying on the sand
I look to the sea
A calmness I feel
A calmness in me

Is this the way that Heaven feels
It doesn't feel right
It doesn't feel real
It feels like a dream
I don't want to awake

Bleeping sounds
Noises, I'm starting to shake
Someone's looking over me
Smiling, talking softly
I'm starting to wake

'It's over,' says one voice
'All things they went well'
But I whisper so quietly,
'Are there things you can tell?'

Where have I been
Where did I go
I cannot remember
I wish I could know

'The operation, remember'
Four hours it took
I need to see
I struggle to look

The bleeping, the noises
All over the place
I struggle to reach
I can't feel my face

There's wires and cables
Now I remember
'What's the date?' I ask softly
It's the ninth of November

I close my eyes
For finally over
Is the date I have been dreading
The ninth of November

I slowly drift off
I'm back on the sand
With the calm, cool sea air
And the sun on my hands

Dreams

Dreams and aspirations
They keep a heart alive
They keep the mind awakened
They make you want to strive

The strive in yourself
The will to achieve
It makes you feel good
The will to believe

Belief in yourself
The belief all around you
The belief in the children
To be who they want to be

To be who they are
To be what they intend
Is the message I give
Is the message I send

The love in yourself
The love all around you
It will give you the will
To do what you intend to do

Live the dream
Let intentions be free
Aspiration and motivation
Believe what you see

The things that you see
For yourself and for others
For these are the things
That in life keep you going

These are the motivations
That in life will keep growing
If only you let them
For then they will grow

For only giving them the chance
Will only they know

As Time Goes By

Time goes so quickly
Yet in the blink of an eye
Before you know what's happening
In front of you stands
Your whole life before you
In some other's hands

Sometimes you may feel
Like control, you have none
Before you even notice
Another year gone

'Another year gone,'
I hear you say
But another brand new one
Will be good, if it may

Think 'half full'
Not 'half empty'
That way you'll have plenty
The good things in life
Your way they will come
Any bad things that have passed
They will come undone

Think future, not past
These days they will last
Will last if you try
As the hours go by

In The Blink Of An Eye

No more a little cherub
This cherub is grown
These wings they have spread
The nest has been flown

The nest, it lies empty
One time was so full
Peaceful and quiet
Now it lies still

The cherubs grew quickly
In the blink of an eye
The years went so quickly
What happened to time?

The time was not to stay still
For the time went so fast
The memories are here
The memories will last

The dusty old albums
Tucked away in the drawers
With the hundreds of photos
Of time stood so still
Photos in frames along the window sill

The photos may fade
The memories will not
These memories you have
You forever have got

A New Life

A magical moment
A magical day
This precious new person
Forever to stay

The special warm feeling
Overjoyed and exhilarated
The longing and waiting is finally over
This person, so special, is finally here

As I look down at this person
I shed a small tear
A tear of such happiness
A tear of such joy

The love, the bond with this special new person
Is a bond like no other
I'm finally me
I'm finally a mother

Just For Me

Over the fields
Beyond the big trees
Is a place that means so much
So much to me

It's a place for no other
It's a place that's just mine
It's a place that's been mine
For a very long time

Ever since I was small
I would go there
The sounds and the scenery
The cold, crisp, fresh air

This place has remained special
This place has remained mine
This place has been special
Throughout all my life

It's a place like no other
It's at the back of the house
There's a gate and a shed
Inside, a small mouse

Where I made him a bed
In there he would hide
From next door's black cat
That would watch him so sly

But the mouse would be safe
Of this, I was sure
He would not become victim
To the big, sly, cat's paw

The day came
'Twas the lorry
We all had to go
So I said goodbye to the mouse

I said to beware
Of the big sly cat
His mean and sharp stare

I think of him now
I hope he was safe
In the bed that I made him
In the dark, dusty place

I smile, close my eyes and I hope that he was
I remember that
Over the fields
Beyond the big trees
Is the place that means so much
So much to me

No One Knows

No one knows, I hear them whisper
No one knows, I hear them say
No one knows, they say together
I hear them whisper every day

They whisper softly
They whisper calmly
But now they're shouting
They're looking at me

I try to run
I try to turn
They're everywhere
Of this I have learned

They mean no harm
They only mean good
I know I should go
Really I should

For out of the window
The lonely dark lane
This place seems much better
But really the same

'There is no such thing,'
The people, they say
But I know the truth
I hear them play

The music will play
From morning till night
For tomorrow they'll be gone
When it does come, the light

Stephen Linden-Wyatt

It was just exactly a month before the Christmas of 2003 when I discovered my love of poetry. It was a close friend who suggested that I should try writing poems to express my views. This suggestion came while I was clearing my chest of many issues that disturbed myself. My friend writes poetry as a hobby so I thought I would give it a try.

There are many subjects that I find inspiring. The main is be my love of cats, although some serious topics such as terrorism can be inspiring. I have a love for nature and have respect for each of the four seasons.

I write poetry to help keep myself sane. I have a problem of bottling things up, so because of this I write poetry. Sometimes my work can be controversial but it is my views on life.

I won't write on a topic that I do not know about. One of my poems is about bullies. As a child I received both physical and verbal abuse, so I wrote a poem to try to help other victims. However though, I like to write various subjects, so there is a poem for everyone.

Poetry can be at times rather tongue twisting and very confusing, so it is my desire to write poetry that all can understand.

I would prefer to be writing than watching the TV. It is a skill that I love, and hope that you will enjoy my work.

Why I Write Poetry

Poetry is something that makes
Me glad,
Even though it can be sad.

I write poetry with humour,
Or write about a subject
That is worse than a puma.

Poetry helps me to express myself,
It can have the tone of joy
That is full of wealth.

Poetry is a skill that makes me
Glad,
Even though jealous people
Say it is just a fad.

Sometimes I cannot write,
Even with all my might
But I know that this block
Will soon take fright.

Poetry I love,
It is better than the TV,
Which is on when I look above.

Winter

I am glad I am inside,
When it is wet and windy,
It is warm inside,
Where everyone is cold outside.

When it rains it is so damp,
And my joints feel like a clamp,
If I could stay warm,
I won't be so damp.

I'll switch on the fire,
Which I so admire,
How each flame,
Can keep me from being so cold.
I wish sitting by me, were my very own flame.

Stretching out by the fire is my cat,
Lying on the mat,
I shall give her a pat,
Oh how she is getting so fat.

I view the outside,
And seeing it is cold outside,
I am glad that I'm not homeless,
I'd hate to be stuck outside.

People travel from work,
Looking as if they need a perk,
I bet you, they are cold,
Especially those that look so old.

It is so dark outside,
And it is only the time of four,
Oh how the weather has not stopped
The pour.

It will flood soon,
And no way will I be able
To get the rain out with a spoon,
Oh, if only I could see the moon.

Spring

The flowers are out,
Looking as fresh
As the winter's snow.
Beaming with colour,
The brown soil is no longer dull.

Keen gardeners are out,
Planning the borders
For the summer's crop,
Deciding what they should grow,
As well as deciding which lawn
They should mow.

The garden centres are full
Of plugs,
As well as repellents to kill
Those slugs.

Veg patches are dug
And seeds are sown,
Some call gardener's mugs,
All because it is still cold
When the seeds are sown.

Spring is here,
The nests are made,
Birds singing for joy,
And bunnies here and there,
What a joy to see new life.

What a joy to see spring,
Buds on the trees,
Bright flowers willing to please,
A joy to know that summer
Is next to come.

Summer

The temperature is of thirty,
And the plants are getting thirsty.

Kids are getting dirty,
And hot parents are getting shirty.

The BBQ smell fills the air,
And kids scream, 'I want
to go to the fair.'

The tone of the ice cream van
is near and Dad's fear,
as it might be dear.

The sea makes a splash,
The sand castles smash.
So then the children
and sea clash.

I am with all that is dear,
I'm glad summer is here.

Autumn

The rain is here
And people fear
That winter will soon
Be near.

The winds take flight
And dogs take fright,
As the wind blows
With all its might.

The trees are bare,
No longer showing their flair,
Although children climb
If they dare.

Flowerbeds are brown,
And gardeners frown,
As they have lost their
Floral crown.

A Creature Of Grace

Beautiful fur
Voices like a purr.

Ears so daint
A cat's cry, so faint.

Tail stands alert
Eyes simply alert.

A cat runs in a brace,
But has elegance and grace.

Fur so fine,
This cat is mine.

My Ragdoll Boy

Oh eyes of a handsome blue,
A wonderful coat, not like glue.

A meow in a tone to greet,
Always pleased to meet.

When I am away, he pines,
I cannot believe he's mine.

He's not a cuddly toy
He's my ragdoll boy.

A Cat's Chase

As I step outside,
I see a cat trying to hide,
Ready to pounce
On something I can't
See to announce.
Stalking as if she
Was in a pack.
Using precision timing
So she won't get any flak.
Suddenly there's a crash
With garden pots lying in
A smash.
A mouse runs
This cat runs.
Trying to catch
A creature that is no match.

Bullies

They think they're big
Yet they're worse than pigs.

They beat people up
All because of one fault.
Why do they think that they
Are as important as a gold cup.

They give verbal abuse,
They're pathetic.
That is why they will never
Call a truce.

People only bully for one reason
All to hide a fault,
But remember they're just as
Bad as treason.

They are unhappy,
This is why they cause you grief,
Unless this changes,
This will never cease.
Although I'm sure you will soon
Get peace.

Don't let them win,
Remember you're better than a bin.
Don't lose soul,
As you're better on the whole.

Remember you are bigger,
So don't try to figure
What makes them trigger!

What Is Friendship?

Friendship is a bond,
Where two people are fond.

Friendship is a love
And should be as pure
As a white dove.

Friendship is special
Something that should
Be kept treasured.

Friendship is about being there,
Where you are close or not.

But one thing for sure
Is that we are close.

We are there for you
And you are here for us,
That is what friendship
Is about.

Love, peace, a strong bond
A treasure.

Our friendship, we will
Always treasure,
And being your friend
Is always a pleasure.

Immoral

Young ladies are pregnant,
They think it's easy to get pregnant.

Education isn't easy,
So they become easy.

A free house,
But isn't this being a mouse.

Many benefits on offer
But no posh food to scoffer.

What happens if these benefits are taken away?
Your money making child, will be taken away.

Is there really satisfaction in this?
There is no bliss.

Would it not be good to be educated,
And have a proper job?
You can only wish.

You chose to be immoral,
So don't pretend to be moral.

You chose your path,
So don't blame people if they laugh.

I hope you're not poor
When your child leaves
Or you'll be scrubbing the floors.

The Northern Hemisphere Champs
World Cup 2003

The atmosphere is like lightning
The floodlights are brightening.

The anthems are sung with a roar,
But no man's expectations are poor.

The ball is kicked high,
White shirts, jump high.

The wallabies are wannabees,
But true success is for the white wannabees.

Men covered in blood are down,
But the crowds are never down.

Penalties are scored,
But tries are roared.

England wins,
Yellow shirts binned.

What success for the best.

Special Love

The pulpit stands high,
But the sound is nigh.

People drive,
People arrive.

Spirits are high,
Singing is high.

Sermon drags,
Old women flag.

The temperature is hot,
Just like the teapot.

Biscuits are shared,
God's family share.

Gossip goes on,
The vicar runs on.

But most of all,
I shared the greatness
Of God's love with all.

Spotlight Poets Information

We hope you have enjoyed reading this book - and that you will continue to enjoy it in the coming years.

If you are interested in becoming a Spotlight Poet then drop us a line, or give us a call, and we'll send you a free information pack.

Alternatively if you would like to order further copies of this book or any of our other titles, then please give us a call or visit our website at www.forwardpress.co.uk

Spotlight Poets

Spotlight Poets Information
Remus House
Coltsfoot Drive
Peterborough
PE2 9JX

Telephone: 01733 898102

Email: spotlightpoets@forwardpress.co.uk